GW01238050

Pamela Gormally

Knucklebones and Pegs

Indigo Dreams Publishing

First Edition: Knucklebones and Pegs
First published in Great Britain in 2025 by:
Indigo Dreams Publishing
24, Forest Houses
Cookworthy Moor
Halwill
Beaworthy
Devon
EX21 5UU

www.indigodreamspublishing.com

Pamela Gormally has asserted her right under the Copyright, Designs and Patents Act 1988 to be identified as the author of this work. © Pamela Gormally 2025

ISBN 978-1-912876-93-8

British Library Cataloguing in Publication Data. A CIP record for this book can be obtained from the British Library.

This book is sold subject to the condition that it shall not, by way of trade or otherwise, be lent, re-sold, hired out, or otherwise circulated without the author's and publisher's prior consent in any form of binding or cover other than that in which it is published and without a similar condition including this condition being imposed on the subsequent purchaser.

Designed and typeset in Palatino Linotype by Indigo Dreams.
Cover design created by Ronnie Goodyer
Author Photo by Michelle Fowler Photography, Morpeth

Printed and bound in Great Britain by 4edge Ltd.
Papers used by Indigo Dreams are recyclable products made from wood grown in sustainable forests following the guidance of the Forest Stewardship Council.

To my sister Barbara,
my first reader, for her encouragement,
guidance and love.

Acknowledgements

I would like to thank the editors of the following publications who first published versions of some of these poems: Butchers' Dog. Obsessed With Pipework, Orbis, Milestones (Write Out Loud), The Northern Poetry Library, Diamond Twig, The Dawntreader (Indigo Dreams) and The Cannon's Mouth.

'All The Questions Float Beyond My Reach' won first prize Sonnet or Not 2022, published in The Cannon's Mouth.
'Do You Still Frame Me On Your Desk?' won third prize Hippocrates 2022, published in Hippocrates Anthology 2022.

Heartfelt thanks in particular to Pippa Little who helped me arrange this collection, and to Ellen Phethean, Colette Bryce, Helena Nelson, Geraldine Green and Julie Hogg (Vane Women) for their support and inspirational workshops. My gratitude to Carte Blanche Writers in Newcastle for their friendship in poetry, and to Mary and Stuart Manley and staff at Barter Books for giving me a safe and peaceful place to write. Thanks to Sean O' Brien, W.N Herbert and Cynthia Fuller for their skilful mentoring at Newcastle University.

Grateful Thanks to Dawn Bauling and Ronnie Goodyer for giving me this opportunity and bringing *Knucklebones and Pegs* to life.

Finally, to my husband Henry who cheered me on and my family for their love and support.

Knucklebones and Pegs is Pamela Gormally's debut collection.

CONTENTS

Knucklebones and Pegs

*"Your absence has gone through me
Like thread through a needle.
Everything I do is stitched through with its color."*
~ W.S.Merwin

*"If I keep a green bough in my heart,
the singing bird will come."*
~ Anon.

Knucklebones

Sweet coven crouching low, scabby knees
on cracked pavements, the taste of melting tar

under our nails, we bring them out, display
the jacks as jewels. They give us power,

hunkered down, banished to the triangle beside
the fence, in the asphalt playground where

buffalo boys roam the plain, trampling underfoot.
Our muttered whispers grow while we aim the ball

higher, reaching the roof, the sky, the moon.
I love to practise, the left one cupped, a plaited nest

while the right hand sweeps across the silver hoard,
precise and in control. When night falls, I press

one tiny detonator into my palm, twist spiky points,
scar a tattoo over life and health, to alter fate.

Where I Belong
After Where I'm From by George Ella Lyon

I am from the iron mangle
turning the cranky handle.
Quick! Hand me those pegs.

I am from the pear tree, in the garden
at Chapman House, my arms wrapped round
wire-haired Scamp, aunts and uncles,
the scarlet rooster and the scrabbling hens.
I am from the toffee taste of Virol,
bubbly Lucozade, a red scooter burning
up city pavements. Throwing jacks
beside the tarry kerb to challenge fate.
I am from 'The Green Hills Far Away'
a whistle in an icy bathroom, 'Bye Bye Blackbird'
fading on the wind-up gramophone.
I'm from the steelworks in a country village,
elusive minnows in the Waskerley Beck,
and sixpences from the Coal Board
in a city of seven hills, smoke and steel.
I am from a box of medals, a Burma Cross,
a rusty car key, 'Blue Moon' sung into
a steamed-up mirror.

I am from great-grannie tramping to the Big House
every Monday Washing Day to soak
the linen in the tubs before she does her own.

Listen

You hunt for the pink roses first,
then the white petals, surrounded
by green leaves.
You seem to have a talent for this.
Started young? You rejoice
when you complete

the sandstone walls from scraps
of grey and cream.
You say you could do
without this gift?
You want to send it back?
Listen. You studied hard

to integrate the sides.
First in a white room,
then the blue. Pieces
still go missing. Gaps.
Some bits would fit
in any space. You wrestle

far too long, give up, walk away.
Listen. It is a shadow
on the corner of a leaf,
a whistle from a pavement crack.
Keep walking.

An Absence

A slender heather tweed costume
        turns the corner
into the street where we play.
        A blur of auburn hair
as I stumble at the kerb
      taste doubt –
               Are you my mother?

I might slip back into Ward Five
      iron beds in a line
            waiting
              waiting
    and you there
        not there
an absence   an ache.

 I am losing my balance
      in a confusion
          of strangers
on a white corridor
      a red light humming
 or
            tilted
inside a closed room.

Eiderdown

I slept under green embroidered satin. Plump
with curled feathers and air. It slid and slipped.
Suffocating warmth. *Do not remember*, it said.
A pale triangle crept between the door and
the half-lit landing. A draught blew in, disturbed
the arms of the dressing gown hanging
on the hook. Its shape shifted and grew. Alarmed
the eiderdown sighed off the bed – *Not to be trusted*,
I burrowed down, a dormouse under worn wool,
counted sheep safe in stone-walled fields. I dreamed –
green-gowned men warned me to lie still, eyes cold
above gauze masks. I fled down silent corridors, twisted
right, doubled left looking for the exit. Behind me,
gaining fast, ether breath, a hand reached out to grip
my shoulder. *Wake! Wake up!* I sobbed. The eiderdown
murmured drowsy, *Forget. Sleep well.* Alone, I threw
the cover's weight aside, tiptoed to the window,
drew back curtains that muffled stars. Opened the latch,
a late car turned into the quiet street. A door closed.

Ode to Invisible Disability

You are a frozen rabbit
on a gurney, a disembodied voice
from the next room warning,

Lie still.

A bead of scarlet blood pricked
on a child's thumb, smeared on a dark slide.

You are a hidden scar, a dress yanked down,
your mother's suppressed fury.

Don't tell.

You're the girl who left, sliding off
the green couch, calling *Time*
to tiled waiting rooms, waving to a weary doctor
scribbling jargon in a file.

You're a young girl racing up a playing field,
brandishing a hockey stick, shouting,

Over here.

You are the effort of forgetting,
a shuttlecock by daylight,
a mountaineer in moonlight,

climbing out of windows,
wristband scalding on your skin.

Jounce

Pared down, a grey amulet
locket-shaped hides in a row
of stones and shells thrown
   by the high spring tide.

I hold it in my hand. Thin layers hint —
the river-ripples on the underside
   glint warm to the touch
under a tang of brackish seaweed
   and the cold hit of the sea.

Click open the hinge
and a breeze from the west lifts
  me home to the Waskerley beck
tumble of icy moorland water carousing
  over the sill,
    the slap of water on rock.

Four children balance
   on steppingstones fishing
for minnows, call to each other
   in high persistent voices.
My small hand curls round a flat pebble
tests it for weight and spin.
   One flick of the wrist,
skimming the surface
    it ricochets far out

Rooster

Out by the study door
each morning for infant school,
I crossed the lane to say hello
to the strutting rooster,
stared back into his fierce dark eye,
admired his scarlet comb,
his gallant cock-a-doodle-do.

I stroked the soft brown feathers
of the hens scrabbling
in the yard for yellow grain,
copied their gentle pecks and clucks,

yet I preferred the cockerel for
his intense regard
and the precise way
he extended
        one leg
            then the other.

Scullery

My aunt's voice calls, *Come, I will show you*
how to do, and I am in the outhouse where tiny insects

scull across the wooden draining board. Earwigs
and beetles bearing armour plate, scurry to shelter

in crevices along the stone slabbed floor. A slate roof
mossed with lichen shades this threshold space

where cobwebs drift above the lintel. It smells of damp
and cool earth trod in on boots from the rainy yard.

Aunt takes my hand and shows me how to scrub
the carrot tops, peel paper onion skins and free

the leeks from dark rich soil. She calls again, *Come,*
I'll show you how to care for flowers. We strip the leaves

from Canterbury Bells gathered in the garden, angle a cut
in the hollow stems, steep in pails of icy moorland water.

Saturdays at the Bakery

Late up from tangled sheets, I ran
through suburban streets in plimsolls, jeans,
t-shirt to the West End and Carrick's Bakery.
Breathed in yeast and cinnamon, climbed
the fire escape to the office, undid the bundle
of receipts, totted up each total in my head.
Mental arithmetic: drilled every morning
at my school, 12, 14, 16 times tables. A tick
if numbers balanced. Red pen if not.
Each spike collected by a supervisor, backcombed
beehive and stilettos. The typewriters' click-clack
at the other end of this long room.
                At my side a tall girl, black hair
in a braid, silver bracelets jangled on brown wrists.
One late morning, we clattered down the stairs,
ducked between delivery vans, whistling drivers
to the factory floor. Admired the workers
bearing trays from hot smoking ovens, collected
fresh warm rolls and doughnuts oozing jam.
I lingered in the sunlit yard to light a cigarette,
Anya called out, *Hurry, we'll be late.*
                Invited home, her mother greeted
me in sari silk, small sisters chattering in Hindi,
English. We played Scrabble to the beat of Bhangra.
I tasted biryani, chilli, peppers, the cool pulse of dahl.

A scientist, in love with Bunsen burners
Anya planned to be a doctor. I loved Hamlet,
Much Ado. She would be married by arrangement,
praised the ritual: a wedding under the Mandap canopy,
rice offered by a bride to the fire.
                    I believed in drama,
passion, the telephone slammed in the hall, the kiss
on the iron bridge.
                    We parted at the summer's end.
I took away the scents of cardamom and cumin,
        the brights of lemon, turquoise, dazzling pink.

Linen Dress

I want a linen dress, orange like the shift
I wore, age nineteen, on the vaporetto.
Hot breeze, bare tanned legs, standing
at the rail on the way to The Lido.
A silver and turquoise bracelet jangling on my wrist.
I want to tilt my face towards the sun,
feel how I arrived at Santa Lucia station,
to speed over the blue lagoon,
find Louisa, Cesare, Sylvie, Marta
in an old apartment overlooking a canal
in Cannaregio. Taste olives, tagliatelle
for the first time. Fling open the shutters
in the early morning light, then *fare la spesa*
Silvie and Marta holding my hands,
my few words of Italian, *Ciao, Che Cosa fare?*
Andiamo, Prego growing by the day.

A Shining Knight on Old Elvet

You sleepwalk through the day, a shuttlecock
blown by the breeze over Prebend's Bridge
to lecture halls, Gawain and the Green Knight.
You've lost your voice, don't meet another's gaze.

At night you slip along the landing, climb through windows,
a stubborn ghost roaming the College grounds,
barefoot, blue wristband glittering on your skin.

November. You face the doctor, Doctor John, in a room
above Old Elvet, disappear inside crimson, orange
patterns on the Persian rug, his voice a long way off.
You answer, *Yes*, more often *No*. Agree to meet each week.
Friends ask, *Did he give you pills?* You say *No*.

Wednesday at 11 a.m. you meet again. Gaze
at twisting spirals. You say *Yes*, more often *No*.
He gives you books: Freud, Jung and Erich Fromm.
You read all through the night. Answer questions
on the text. You know how to read a book.
You notice birds and flowers in the margins of the rug.

You meet again with Doctor John in the room above the street.
Through the window you watch fellow students striding past.
You spy a thick file on his desk.
Open at the early pages.

You seem to recognise this file? He lifts his pen.
He marks the page. You hear these words,
Hard to be in hospital when you were three.

Separated –
           from all you love.
No-one to tell your memories to.

You lift your head.
           A child's voice fills the room.

Brief Street

Slipshod in broken strapped sandals
trailing a long flowery skirt, I cut my foot

on glass lying on the scorched June pavement.
I hobbled to the front door, 1 Brief St.

rang the bell, left bloody footprints on the lino floor.
The owner, a startled Miss Leila Davis,

retired from St Gabriel's College, whisked me
past the press of bodies crowding the stairs,

other would-be tenants for the upstairs flat.
She ran cold water in the bath, bathed my foot,

plucked out tiny slivers, wrapped a bandage
before we talked, sitting round her kitchen table.

The deal was sealed when my young man arrived,
they shared a passion for Dostoevsky, Tolstoy,

Solzhenitsyn. I added Anna Akhmatova.
Gulag, betrayal, faith.

That evening we toasted our new home with iced vodka
to the sound of bells calling across deep snow.

Some Doubts
After 'Some Fears' by Emily Berry

Doubt living another year, doubt
open spaces on wide beaches,
doubt bridges suspended between swaying
cliffs, Indiana Jones, doubt stepping
from cars, still on the move,
doubt paving stones, rain-washed
cobbles, the dangerous edge.
Doubt unsettled departure board
at Central Station. *Is that my train?*
Doubt time passing, time stopped.
                    What is the time?
Doubt saying the wrong thing, not
saying the wrong thing, doubt
where to end a line,
doubt endings altogether. Doubt beetroot,
sushi, vinegar. Doubt wind blowing
from the east. Doubt eerie hum
from the old black and white tv. Doubt dis-
appearance of messages
while typing emails –
                    Where do they go? Doubt
vanishing, being held in someone's
mind. Doubt any person in a white coat,
green tiles, fluor-
escent lights. Doubt lifts going
up, lifts going down. *Doors closing.*

All the Questions Float Away Beyond My Reach

You woke at dawn in a sparse mountain hut,
eager to see Sagarmatha, Lord of the Sky,
only to find a white haar covered the ridge.
Damp, cold, obscuring your hand before your face.
You'd trekked through the foothills of Nepal,
the cool light a relief from the heat you endured
in The Forgotten War. I think of that mist you drew
down when I asked you about the past, the rare
glimpse you gave of fear, as pitch-dark fell like
a knife, and the tropical clamour tuned up, concealing
the approach of a kill. I watched as you lathered
your face with a shaving brush, stroking the razor
over your chin, singing *Blue Moon, you saw me
standing alone*, to the hazy reflection in the glass.

Route 261

You mount the top deck, heading south
through London suburbs. Branches tap
at the window, as you leave dusty streets

cluttered with rundown, jumbled buildings
and climb into a tree-lined world.
You walk round a corner, hear a blackbird sing

A long way from Deptford. Guilt and delight
knock together in your divided heart.
No traffic noise, nor sour petrol smell

this spring morning, but daffodils, blue hyacinths.
You miss the cries of market traders,
the sprawl of workshop tools, and bales of cloth

spilling indigo and scarlet over city pavements.
Yet the blackbird sings, and the apple tree waves drifts
of blossom, and you walk through gates thrown wide –

no locked school yard. Surprised, an upper window opens,
a stranger's voice calls out your name.

Mrs Silver Polishes Her Thoughts

One last trip, you promised as you hurled
your cutlass and skillet into the sea chest.
Elbow deep in soap suds, eyes stinging
I refused to turn round. So, you started singing
in your rusty bucket voice:

I'll be back before you know it, before
the leaves turn gold and waves crest silver
up the Bristol Channel.

As soon as I caught sight of that fox-eyed
boy, I knew he would be trouble.
No, you blustered. *The lad has spirit, reminds*
me of myself when I was young.
Exactly, I said as I carried pots to the yard.

You're crowing like a rooster through the open
window, while I'm feeding the scrabbling hens,
you're tossing brandy, a pistol under the blanket.

We will ride together through London streets.
I'll toast you, my lady, in ruby wine.
We'll feast on guinea hen and partridge.

So many promises. Last night you winked,
told me there was a map and treasure,
fell asleep with your head on my breast.

                    *

Of course, it was the wrong island.
Desolate pine swept down to the strand,
no palm tree to wave welcome

like my dear country, where surf boomed
under a dazzling sun, but treacherous
swamp, where you camped under a Hunter's Moon.

The sun's diluted here, like adding water to rum.
Polishing a tankard in The Spyglass snug,
I spy light sparkling on a turquoise sea.

Squire Trelawney and Doctor Livesey returned
battle hardened, treasure rich, Jim Hawkins feted
as a hero, but you, you've disappeared –

I sold the inn, moved east to Tilbury docks. Still ripe,
I long for your swaggering tongue and honey bravado.
I am waiting for a word. Send me a word –

I'll be back before you know it, before
      the leaves turn gold and waves crest silver
                  up the Bristol Channel...

On the Way to the Bus Stop

we meet Raymond, loping along, hood up,
absent for three weeks. *We're going to the Tower,*
Bertram says, black hair springing
from his beanie. *Want to come?*
Raymond shrugs into the pavement cracks.
Crammed onto the no.78 top deck, we leave
The Old Kent Road, swing through Southwark
warehouses, cross the bridge that spans
the river.
            We file through Traitor's Gate, avoid
the spikes, dazzled by the jewels in the keep.
A beefeater in splendid red and gold, prods
Catherine with his halberd, as she shades in each
piece of chainmail. *I can't believe her concentration,*
Bertram's freehand swoops across his paper. Bold
strokes carve the guard. Underneath Raymond's faint
pencil lines a story saunters: a knight, a quest,
a lady, and betrayal. We race past the ravens strutting on
the 'Keep Off' lawn, to embankment benches, breeze
fresh from the river, a smoky scent, diesel, soot,
share packed rolls, apples. Seagulls dive for crumbs.
Turn our faces to the sun as the bridge divides and lifts,
hoot when the tugboat steers a ship to open sea.
            When we get back, school yard in sight,
Bertram calls, *See you tomorrow.* Raymond peels away.

Art Trolley

My lace-up shoes click-clacking,
I wheel the metal trolley down the corridor,
past institutional pale green tiles.

Inside the classroom I dispense
pencils, pastels, charcoal, arrange a still life,
thistles, sheep skull, an abalone shell.

Watch me children, I'll show you how
criss-cross shading creates darkness, light.
We use magnifiers to enlarge the marks
on feathers, shells, and bones.

I guide their hands, with curved blades
we incise a wren, an ant, a blade of barley
into the soft muscle of pale brown lino.

We pour bright inks, scarlet, lemon, turquoise
into printing trays, roll colour across ridges,
then press the tablets onto quiet paper.

Leaping images glow in their startled eyes.

Cranefly

When I leap – my long legs scissoring
    across the cool white tiles
float past your startled gaze
      my lace wings caressing
    your restless hair –
      do not flinch
or be alarmed.
                  I am Nijinsky!
 Admire me
      while I strike
       an attitude croisée devant.

Applaud my grand allegro
          when I spring
    across the wooden floor, fling
        a final grand jeté
       wild
         from the ceiling.

Spectaculaire, they called – *Diabolique!*
      Is that why you fear me?

I exist on air.
    Blown in
        from Polish grasslands
grandson of circus artists
       attracted
        to the lights

I burn on stage.
         In Paris I danced
                  The Rite of Spring
                  and flared a riot.

Now, on late September nights
                  I dance for you alone
         my graceful coda,
                  my leap of risk –
                           The Rite of Autumn.

Dragonfly Nymph

Lean twig lying on the mud, hidden
until it begins to move at speed, propelling
mean body on oars that scull the water, raise
a cloud of dust, a dark tornado.
      From the centre, the mask shoots
a steel trap, impales a water flea, or a half-formed
tadpole, unable to break free. We can't look.
We watch, as it disappears in spiked gulps.
The twig lies still again, submerged.
Above, the pond water looks clear, undisturbed.
      A skin-shedder, discarding carapace
ten times, leaves hollow parcels, lost property,
evidence around the edges of the pond.
      A mud and sand dweller, through
two harsh winters, in May, when birds build
their nests, it makes a slow, determined climb
from cool water on to a green stem, rests
      in the evening air. Under a pin-prick
scattering of stars the head cracks open –
like a walnut.
      A new creature slides out trembling,
vulnerable, resembling her early name *Nymph*, warms
in the sun. Compound eyes take in new elements, light
and air, register the slightest movement. Dancing
above the natal pond, the dragonfly, iridescent blue.

Adele and the Moon Moth

Towards noon, Adele whispers *Look,*
lifting her hand to reveal a Moon Moth
resting its papery wings on her warm fist.

Under the palm fronds inside the tropical Glass House,
the children's astonished cries hushed
by humid heat and the sight of countless moths
and butterflies fluttering between tall green plants,
Eugenia and Eucalyptus towering over their small heads.

Madagascan Moon Moth folds luminous lemon-yellow wings,
paper-thin painted fans. Long feathery streamers hang
from Adele's small knuckle.
Large brown eyes smudged with blue irises,
stroked on at each wing's edge, become reflected light
in the small girl's widened pupils.
They warn any careless predator,
I am even larger and more dangerous than you imagine.

Dipping her wings in salute, she shimmers away, a comet
trailing streamers that would blaze across the midnight sky
in Madagascar, her island home, under a silver moon.

Now at noon, she swings up high,
vanishes inside the enchanted glass house.

Oarweed's Tangle

The marsh grass sways behind the dunes,
hush-a-bye in the evening sun.
In the hollows a dusting of blue harebells,
soothe-a-rue, soothe-a-rue,
stubble of rose-pink thrift cushions the rise.

As I climb the dunes, I hear the sea
                    its drawn out *haaagh* –
In this new-found land javelins hurled
by angry gods in winter storms,
basalt glittering, punished
by a sea pulse into Neolithic tools.
Oarweed's dark tangle;
                    bleached bladderwrack.

A wave lifts and dunks
a sour pebble deep in a rock pool;
diving for cover a green shore crab clings
to sliding carragheen.
Waves' undertow pulls back regrets
                    drag-drash, drag-drash
reluctance, reluctance
                    drawn out *haaagh*

The Train at 8.03

Alnmouth to Newcastle, a northern burr
calls for tickets, gone before I find my wallet.

You're tucked out of sight behind the senior railcard,
old season ticket, folded into quarters, date smudged, obscured.
You taste of coffee, heat, and city pavements.

I slide you back, gaze at rowan trees, bent by wind,
turbines skirling in a Shepherd's Warning Sky.

Newcastle Central Station: I wait on Platform 4,
commuters surge away, briefcases held high, the train
departs for London. In my mind a distant tannoy chants,
Hither Green to London Bridge and Platform 5.

You summon me to work, old season ticket, my driven purpose,
as I cross the river to my school. You sing
to me in children's fifty different accents,
We are the World. Don't forget us.

Today, I climb the iron stairs, one step at a time.
At the exit I thrust this morning's ticket into the machine's
tetchy mouth. Hesitate –

Should I plunge you too inside?
                    Would you disappear?

Tinnitus

Tinderbox: flint and tinder rasp steel.
Inside a dark cave a flame splutters,
boots click – *Eyes-as-big-as-saucers* leaps
and growls, pickaxes – pk pk pound blows
on rough stone. A crow's beak peck pecks
soft tissue down to bone; six shrieks
from a tin whistle howl an owl's warning.
A tincture of hebenon drives the mind into
a tizz of terror; an old woman shouts loss
on a sparse heath. A Cornish wheel grinds
silvery tin under a roaring cliff, a wave fills
a curved shell to pressure point; a tinker flings
distracting rings, currents of air displaced
fraught. A conniving curse. Jail and Clink.

(Note: Hebenon was the poison Claudius dropped into Hamlet's
father's ear.)

Seeds

The junior radiologist brings out a box,
holds it at arm's length. She wears a mask
and heavy-duty gardening gloves.

A new sound fills the room— click click,
crickets in dry grass among the dunes.
A breeze from the sea lifts the curtain,
a tang of iodine and salt.

I laugh. The consultant chides,
This is a pioneering treatment. These seeds
will light the surgeon along the path.

I see two small figures walk hand in hand
through a darkening forest.

The procedure quick. A sharp scratch
twice as the crickets plunge inside my skin.

I ask to see the screen. There they are:
two pulsing lights,
one above the nipple at midnight,
a dark centre.
　　　　　And the other flickers
in the suspect cells to the far left –
a long row of tiny dots traced above a wave.

Passport

Staff Nurse Sue hands me a duplicate
yellow form. *The last thing before you go,* echoes
as I cross the foyer, pass the bee-sting flower stall,
the humming escalator, hear the creak of signs
for x-ray, E.C.G. burrow deeper and deeper into
the ship's hold, until I find The Hall of Lifts.
Full Stop. *Don't forget to breathe.*
Pressed behind a woman on a stretcher, a porter
and two doctors locked in consultation, we ascend
spilling out on Level Five, when I sway down
the longest deck to Ward 45, opposite an airless cabin,
where Clare unrolled the book of charts and diagrams.
Along the way I wonder, *How good to have this
medical advance* – a passport photograph stamped
on an identity card, pinned to your gown. No need
for constant questions: *Your name? Your date of birth?*
No need for the empty wristband.

                         I reach the door
marked *Post the Form and Knock.*
As the clock strikes two a young girl hangs my coat,
asks me to wait. That gives me time
to comb my hair, dishevelled, seasick
from the patient morning, the tramline marking up.
In the silver mirror I paint my lips a deep plum,
apply mascara. I want to look my best.

A woman appears, a heavy camera
strapped round her neck. She gives her name,
Jessica. I give her mine. We smile ready for the shot.
She tells me to step over to the full-length screen.
Stand on X.
As I move forward, before the shutter falls,
                  she calls out, *Take off your top.*
                       Don't forget to breathe.

Shirring

Orange wire, taut,
tugs me awake in the early hours,
sends an echo depth-charged.

A moonbeam sneaks
inside the blind, props open
my glazed eyelids

whispers *Look* —
traces the neater breasts,
circles the missing nipples,

the shirred line of stitches,
fastens hooks
along my back, wraps

a piece of lint inside the band
to ease the strain.
Then leaves, exit left

through the casement window.
In the starless dark
a heaviness, a weight, a lack.

Honesty *(Lunaria annua)*

A large jug with a broad rim,
a band of leaves at the base,
traced in muted colours
       a crackle in the glaze.
It held a spray of honesty,
oval seed heads, paper-thin,
gleamed with an eerie light.

In spring, orange-tip butterflies
laid their eggs on the green leaves.
In winter, each time the door opened
       on the porch
silver pods shivered in the draught.

Honesty 2

My mother stands by the window
in her cream dress, printed with petals,
            white hair, once auburn,
still springy to the touch.
She waves goodbye while I turn
the corner in the cool February light
            to the branch line
country station, express train to the city.

The night before, she reads aloud
the news in the local paper. Someone
            who lived in the old house
at the top of the hill,
has been taken to court, found guilty
            of child abuse.
A respectable member of the community.

The spring in my throat unlocks.
Words leap from my mouth.
So long a silence. The Lift. The porters
            at the children's hospital.

She stares at me. Her voice shakes.
Fetch the sherry from the cupboard.
A small glass for both of us, gulped down.
Amber liquid clouding tears.

Will

I will not step inside the lift.
I will not lie down.
I will not look.
I will not cower, cry or shake.
I will not listen to your words.
I am not your *princess*,
or your *sweetheart*.
I will not watch the doors.

I will stride out in the cool air.
I will notice lime green moss.
Listen to the blackbird's song.
I will shake my head free.
I will claim back those words.
I will delight in acting like a princess.
I will glory in my own sweet heart.

My Mother's Wallet

Deep inside a pocket, tucked
in an old leather suitcase, I found
a small wallet in the broom cupboard
under the stairs.

I brought it to the light –
claimed it as my own, palm-sized,
a cherished missal, midnight blue
stiff mottled skin with darker circles,
tiny crystals formed from ice. They burn.

I scooped out faded
appointment cards marked in red
and two formal letters,
one confirming treatment
at the Marie Curie Clinic,
with a handwritten postscript
from the Ward Sister –
We send our love to Pamela.

Dates, records, names are all revealed,
a wave calling –
Here we are, we remember you.

Wristband

I wrote my name on slate
with a piece of chalk,
left-handed
against my nature —
the name no longer mine
since first inscribed
on narrow band encircling
my child wrist
to remind them
who I was
before they lifted
me from my cot-bed
and checked again,
What is your name?
The name that carried me
inside the closing lift,
the name salivated
by the porters at my back,
the name starched
in accusation,
the name murmured
by the doctor as he pulled me under.

Orange

Sister stands starched white,
grips the rail
at the foot of my cot-bed.
Shouts, *You Wicked Girl!*
Nil by Mouth!

Strips of orange peel,
discarded pith,
gleam on black and white tiles
in the light from high windows.

Across the ward my friend,
small boy in the opposite bed, smiles.
We laughed when he threw the peel.

Sister's voice rises to the edge of panic.
Why did you eat the orange?
Who gave you the orange?

Do You Still Frame Me On Your Desk?

When the doctors told my mother
Prepare yourself. All hope is lost,
my unassuming father caught
a tram to Sheffield Children's Hospital
and demanded to see *The Main Man*

and that was you, Mr Anderson,
a burly fellow in a white coat
and a stethoscope that told me
breathe in, breathe out –
and you said, *There's always hope.*
We'll give it our best shot.
You chose the scalpel, drove the blade
deep into the skin, closed the wound
with a fine needle. A skilful putt.

All my childhood I looked back
to see you painting violet dye
on my tender side
while I perched high on the hard table,
aged three, so nearly four.
The cold stroke of the brush tickled
and I laughed out loud. You laughed too,
a bear's deep growl.
Behind you, all the junior doctors
clustered, attentive,
their serious faces dissolving into mirth.

Drystone Wall

The stones on the top ridge
slant towards the setting sun,
aubergine and rose,
cushioned by sphagnum moss
and lichen starred with crimson petals.
At the centre, larger stones hold fast
through wind and rain and mid-life hail,
while emerald, sage and olive spill
from crevices; at the base
lie limestone slabs and rubble,
and fits and starts of boulders,
roots overgrown with ferns,
nettles. A tangle of purple loosestrife
winds up the wall. Just there,
you find a gap between the stings,
where a young field mouse might
scramble through from field to lane.

Tai Haku

My pulse slows. Along a winding path I climb
to the cherry orchard. Petals blizzard down

as the breeze shakes the branches, opening and closing,
pleated silk fans. A girl swings between two posts,

wild hyacinths and tulips at her feet. Rooks call
an answer from the pine trees in the distance.

A butterfly shimmers past, her wings the colour
of the parchment lanterns hanging at the entrance,

Japanese calligraphy brushed on by survivors.
I remember how my father, who wore the Burma Star,

and the visitor from Japan exchanged gifts long
after the war, a blue Wedgewood vase, a crimson silk kimono.

The plash and slip of water over the rills.
Brief season, delayed
                    by a harsh winter –
                                        a girl swings.

(Tai Haku cherry trees planted in Alnwick Gardens.
This tree was lost in Japan, discovered in an English Garden
and then restored to Japan.)

Field Guide

We walk the bounds, late September afternoon.
The day before, a tractor drove through the gate,
mowed down the grasses that danced in the wind.
Purple feathered stalks hiding field mice, insects
and bees. Were some caught in the blades?

A young blackbird darts ahead along the track,
pauses – every few yards, his yellow beak scratches
in the turned earth for worms. Whistles, *Keep Up!*
A rhythm sets up in our walking – our terrier potters
behind, a spurt and she jogs past. She's not done yet.

Clouds blow across the darkening sky, late sun
casts shadows. The cries of children racing down
the pitch echo in the dusk. The field is waiting –
developers will arrive with yellow diggers,
change the old school into luxury homes.
The avenue of lime trees planted a century ago,
still stands, dense foliage turning gold.

The sky blazes crimson at the last corner,
our field guide leaves, vanishing –
into the undergrowth, a warning whistle.
The following day, when we return,
we find the five-barred gate padlocked.
A new sign hangs, *Private Land.*

The Causeway

Loop thin string
over serrated edges,
tie a knot
to hold the tension fast.
Thread a bodkin
with rough pink and grey
for stubborn ruins.
Leave gaps for celeste blue,
a wisp of white for dizzy clouds.
Tease undyed wool, soft
through the warp –
a flock of sheep grazing
on knotty olive turf.
Weave a lemon silk
for the wave-scoured shore –
chase dots of indigo
pilgrims' footsteps.
Then twist a turquoise
with a strand of pewter
for the cry of terns,
the toss of waves.
Add a tiny cowrie shell,
a feather from a sanderling,
a blade of marram grass
to hook the texture
of wind and salt.

January

Rowan branches shiver in the wind,
lit by a lamp's reflection

through half-closed shutters.
Headstrong, you push into a squall,

bend downhill towards the fire blazing
in the Blue Waiting Room. The wind scours

your skin, tosses autumn rags
into the gutter, ruffles

the surface of puddles. Blows
your umbrella inside out –

silver spikes frame an unexpected view.

When you return, the rowan tree still stands,
curls roots into the earth, bare branches in the storm.

Winter light pours honey down the terrace.

Tray

Those days of illness and recovery
my mother carried a tray to my room.
An egg, soldiers of buttered toast.
A glass of Lucozade, bubbles of energy.
I lay in bed, hot fever raging. She bathed
my forehead, slid the silver bulb
under my tongue, straightened pillows,
rang the doctor who came at midnight
with his leather bag.

I took all this for granted. Waited
for my father to come home from work,
to move the counters along the board, sail
galleons across the sea to Treasure Island.
My mother cooked the supper,
helped with homework, washed and ironed.
Did I thank her?
All those days and nights of worry.
How the lines began to crease,
how her breath began to hurry.

Now I would bring her this enamelled tray,
a silver teapot, a china cup,
a plate with lemon drizzle cake,
a tiny vase of yellow primroses,
like the ones she picked, a country girl
by the railway cutting.

Pegs

Blue sky, white scudding clouds,
a western breeze blows up the dale. I space

rinsed-clean sheets along the line, taut
at the corners as she showed me when a child,

to hail the wind and sail the blue horizon.
Each peg a memory: across the kitchen table

we drew faces, stitched cloaks from velvet scraps,
gave each figure a name, a voice to fit the tales

she knew by heart. Now I stand in her summer garden
at the top note of my scale in health and strength,

while she descends in a minor key, so frail,
yet as she steps out through the garden door

A Grand Day, she calls, and hoists the prop to lift
the line out further and catch the freshening breeze.

Pilgrim Rose

Petals must fall.

A fragile stem supports a full flower.

Thorns offer a handhold.

At the heart of the universe is the spiral.

*

This is the rose
            you chose in The Gardens,
for the name and the scent,
            that you grew in a pot,
no space on the walls,

this is the rose
            tied loose to tall stakes
to protect from the wind
            that blows from the coast,
in the far north of our land,

this is the rose twisting over the spikes
            of the dark copper shrub,
gleaming starlight within
            grey-green Astrantia,
'flower of the moon',

this is the rose
        you water each evening,
that bears creamy buds
        that fold into blossoms
above thorns that do prick,

if you don't take due care –
        Don't Fall Asleep!

This is the rose spilling petals in spirals,
        from buttery yellow
to ivory lace, to a pale milky-white
        dotted with crimson,
                flushed in glory.
This is the Pilgrim Rose.

Indigo Dreams Publishing Ltd
24, Forest Houses
Cookworthy Moor
Halwill
Beaworthy
Devon
EX21 5UU
www.indigodreamspublishing.com